2ND EDITION

THE **BIG BOOK** OF
ROCK

PIANO · VOCAL · GUITAR

ISBN 0-793-51434-7

HAL·LEONARD®
CORPORATION
7777 W. BLUEMOUND RD. P.O. BOX 13819 MILWAUKEE, WI 53213

Visit Hal Leonard Online at
www.halleonard.com

CONTENTS

ALL RIGHT NOW

Words and Music by PAUL RODGERS
and ANDY FRASER

BAD CASE OF LOVING YOU

Words and Music by
JOHN MOON MARTIN

Whoa.

I know you like ___ it.

You like it on top.

Tell me ma-

AQUALUNG

Music by IAN ANDERSON
Lyrics by JENNIE ANDERSON

Faster

BABE, I'M GONNA LEAVE YOU

Words and Music by ANNE BREDON,
JIMMY PAGE and ROBERT PLANT

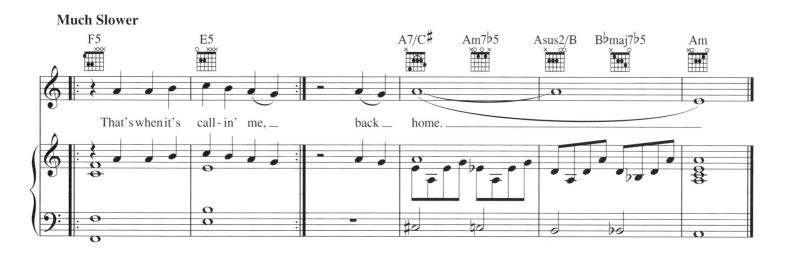

That's when it's call-in' me, __ back __ home. _____

Additional Lyrics

I know, I know, I know, I never, I never, I never, I never, I never leave you, baby
But I got to go away from this place, I've got to quit you.
Ooh, baby, baby, baby, baby
Baby, baby, baby, ooh don't you hear it callin'?
Woman, woman, I know, I know it's good to have you back again
And I know that one day, baby, it's really gonna grow, yes it is.
We gonna go walkin' through the park every day.
Hear what I say, every day.
Baby, it's really growin', you made me happy when skies were grey.
But now I've got to go away
Baby, baby, baby, baby
That's when it's callin' me
That's when it's callin' me back home...

BACK IN THE U.S.S.R.

Words and Music by JOHN LENNON
and PAUL McCARTNEY

Moderate Rock tempo

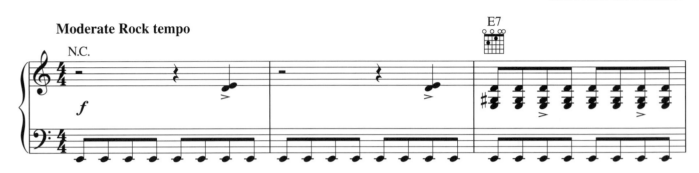

Flew in from Mi - a - mi Beach, B.
Been a - way so long I hard - ly
Show me 'round your snow - peaked moun - tains

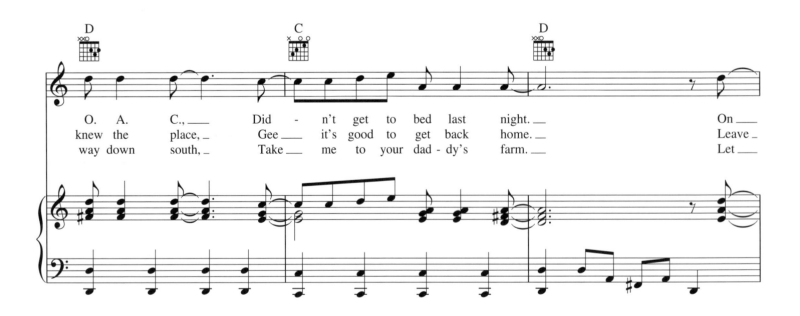

O. A. C., ___ Did - n't get to bed last night. ___ On ___
knew the place, ___ Gee ___ it's good to get back home. ___ Leave ___
way down south, ___ Take ___ me to your dad - dy's farm. ___ Let ___

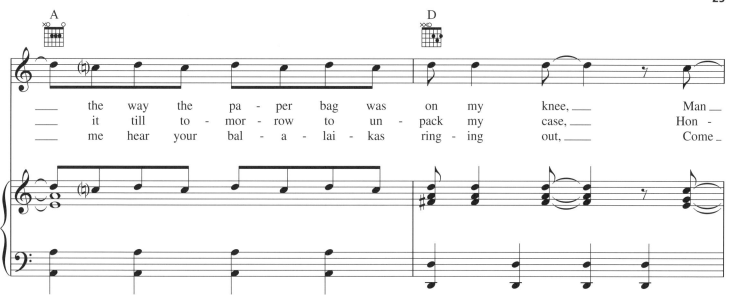

the way the pa - per bag was on my knee, ___ Man ___
it till to - mor - row to un - pack my case, ___ Hon -
me hear your bal - a - lai - kas ring - ing out, ___ Come _

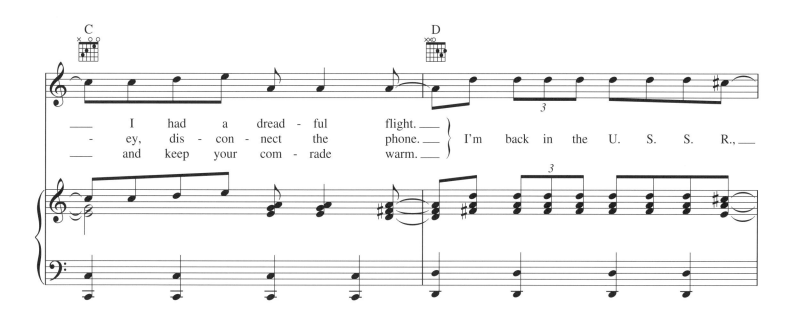

___ I had a dread - ful flight. ___ } I'm back in the U. S. S. R., ___
- ey, dis - con - nect the phone. ___ }
___ and keep your com - rade warm. ___ }

To Coda

You don't _ know how luck - y you are, ___ boy. ___

BEAST OF BURDEN

Words and Music by MICK JAGGER
and KEITH RICHARDS

BORN TO BE WILD

Moderate Rock

Words and Music by
MARS BONFIRE

Get your mo-tor run-ning,_____ Head out on the high - way_____
I like smoke and light - ning,_____ heav - y met - al thun - der_____

___ ing look - ing for ad - ven - ture in what
___ ing rac - ing in the wind_____ and the

ev - er comes our way._____
feel - ing that I'm un - der._____ Yeah, dar - ling, gon - na

nev - er want to die._____ Born   to be   wild.__

_____ Born   to be wild.__

Born   to be   wild._____

Repeat and Fade

BRAIN DAMAGE

Words and Music by
ROGER WATERS

The pa - per holds their fold - ed fac - es to the floor, _ and ev - 'ry day _ the pa - per boy _ brings more. And if the dam _ breaks o - pen man - y years too soon, _ and if there is no room up - on _ the hill, _

THE BOYS ARE BACK IN TOWN

Words and Music by
PHILIP PARRIS LYNOTT

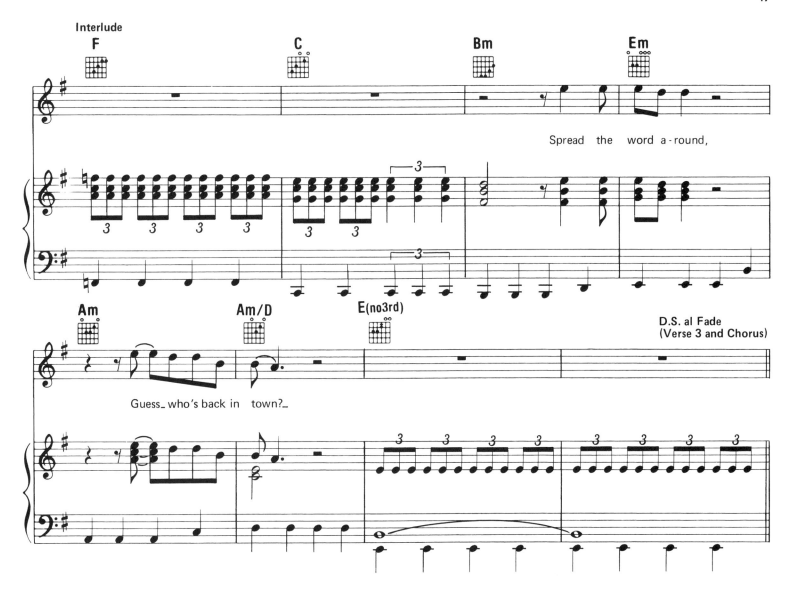

Additional Verses:

2. You know that chick that used to dance a lot
   Every night she'd be on the floor shaking what she'd got
   Man, when I tell you she was cool, she was hot
   I mean she was steaming.

   And that time over at Johnny's place
   Well, this chick got up and she slapped Johnny's face
   Man, we just fell about the place
   If that chick don't wanna know, forget her.

   (Chorus & Interlude)

3. Friday night they'll be dressed to kill
   Down at Dino's Bar and Grill
   The drink will flow and blood will spill
   And if the boys want to fight, you better let 'em

   That jukebox in the corner blasting out my favorite song
   The nights are getting warmer, it won't be long
   It won't be long till summer comes
   Now that the boys are here again.

   (Chorus and Fade)

BREAKDOWN

Words and Music by
TOM PETTY

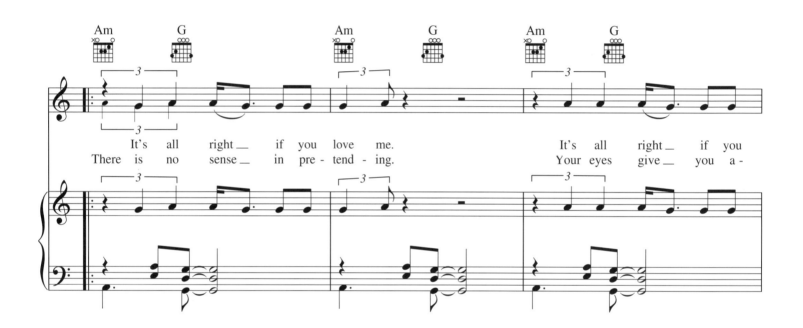

It's all right __ if you love me.
There is no sense __ in pre-tend-ing.

It's all right __ if you
Your eyes give __ you a-

don't. __
way. __

I'm not a-fraid of you run-ning a-way hon-ey,
Some-thing in-side you is feel-ing like I do. __

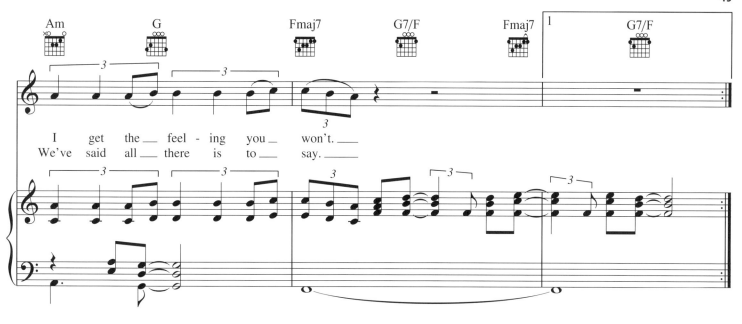

I get the __ feel - ing you __ won't. ___
We've said all __ there is to __ say. _____

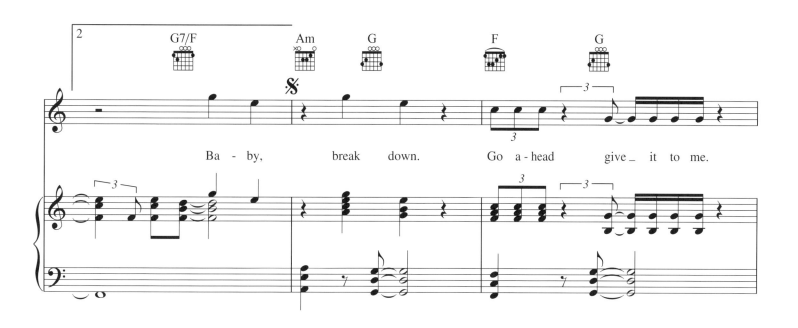

Ba - by, break down. Go a - head give __ it to me.

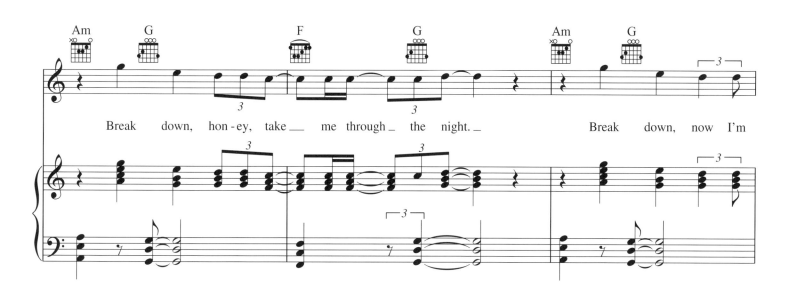

Break down, hon - ey, take __ me through __ the night. __ Break down, now I'm

stand-in' here, can't you see? __ Break down, it's all right, __

it's all right, it's all right.

BROWN EYED GIRL

Words and Music by
VAN MORRISON

Additional Lyrics

2. Whatever happened to Tuesday and so slow
Going down the old mine with a transistor radio
Standing in the sunlight laughing
Hiding behind a rainbow's wall
Slipping and a-sliding
All along the water fall
With you, my brown eyed girl
You, my brown eyed girl.
Do you remember when we used to sing:
Chorus

3. So hard to find my way, now that I'm all on my own
I saw you just the other day, my, how you have grown
Cast my memory back there, Lord
Sometime I'm overcome thinking 'bout
Making love in the green grass
Behind the stadium
With you, my brown eyed girl
With you, my brown eyed girl.
Do you remember when we used to sing:
Chorus

CALL ME

from the Paramount Motion Picture AMERICAN GIGOLO

Words by DEBORAH HARRY
Music by GIORGIO MORODER

Col - or me __ your col - or, ba - by, col - or me __ your car. __ Col - or me __ your col - or, dar - ling, I know who __ you are. __

CARRY ON

Words and Music by
STEPHEN STILLS

64

what you do ___ and what ___ you see, ___ lov - er can ___ you talk ___

___ to me? ___

2nd time D.S. and Fade

CAN'T GET ENOUGH

Words and Music by
MICK RALPHS

nough of your love. _____

CENTERFOLD

Written by SETH JUSTMAN

Does she walk?__ Does she talk?__ Does she come com - plete?__ My
It's o - kay, __ I un - der - stand, __ this ain't no nev - er nev - er land. I

home-room, home-room an - gel al - ways pulled me from my seat
hope that when this is - sue's gone, I'll see you when your clothes are on.

COLD AS ICE

Words and Music by MICK JONES
and LOU GRAMM

some-day you'll pay.

Cold as

COLD SHOT

Words and Music by MIKE KINDRED
and WESLEY CLARK

1. Once was a sweet thing, ba - by. We held our love in our hands.
2. Re-mem-ber the way that you loved me. You'd do an-y-thing I said.
3. *Instrumental solo ad lib.*

But now I reach to kiss your lips, my touch don't mean a thing.
But now I see you out some - where, you won't give me the time of day.

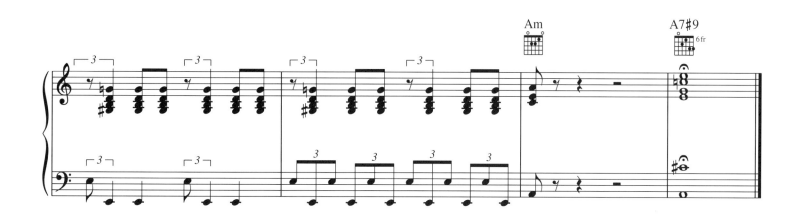

CRAZY ON YOU

Words and Music by ANN WILSON,
NANCY WILSON and ROGER FISHER

Cra - zy on you. Let me go

cra - zy, crazy on you,_____ oh. _____ Your

oh. _____

Wild man's_ world is cry - ing in pain. What - cha gon - na do__ when ev - 'ry-

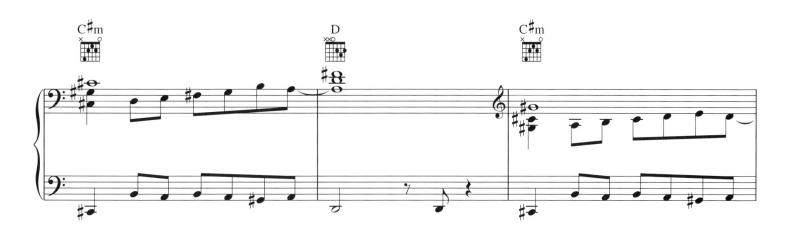

CROCODILE ROCK

Words and Music by ELTON JOHN
and BERNIE TAUPIN

CUTS LIKE A KNIFE

Words and Music by BRYAN ADAMS
and JIM VALLANCE

DO YOU FEEL LIKE WE DO

Words and Music by PETER FRAMPTON, JOHN SIOMOS,
RICK WILLS and MICK GALLAGHER

DUST IN THE WIND

Words and Music by
KERRY LIVGREN

Moderate Folk style

EVERYBODY PLAYS THE FOOL, SOMETIME

Words and Music by RUDY CLARK,
KENNY WILLIAMS and J.R. BAILEY

EVIL WOMAN

Words and Music by
JEFF LYNNE

124

FEELIN' ALRIGHT

Words and Music by
DAVE MASON

FIRE AND ICE

Words and Music by TOM KELLY,
SCOTT SHEETS and PAT BENATAR

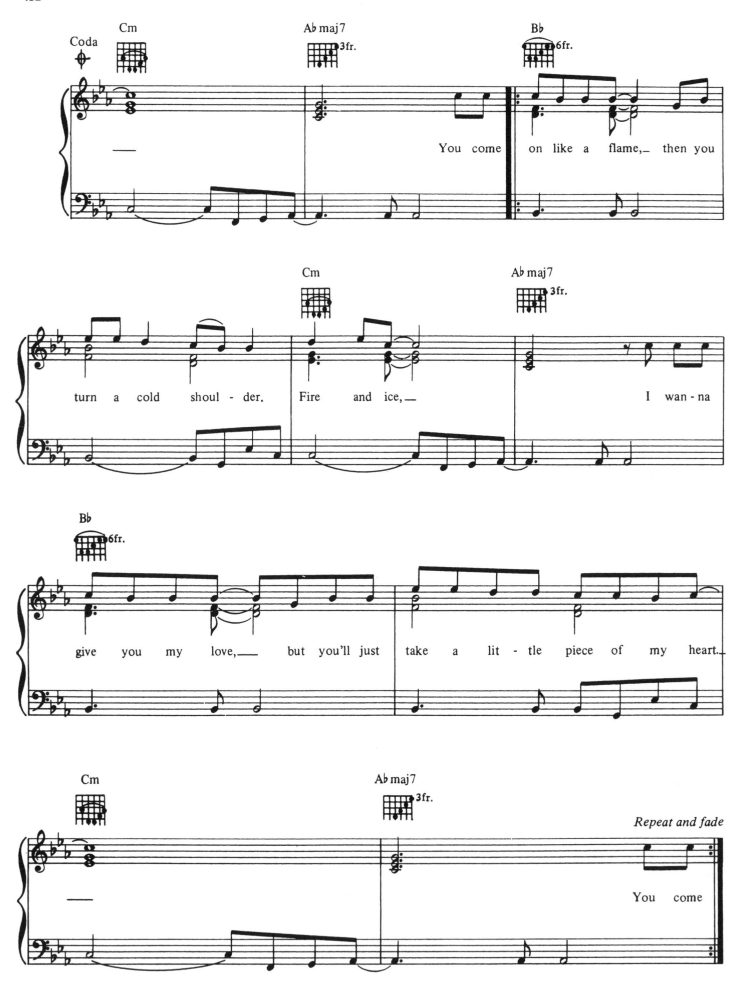

FREE BIRD

Words and Music by ALLEN COLLINS
and RONNIE VAN ZANT

Moderately slow

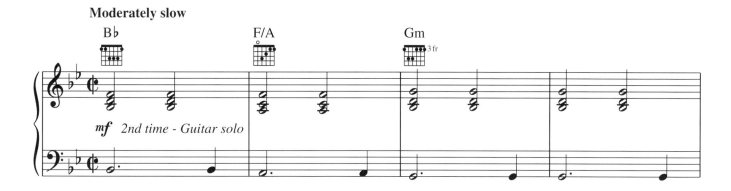

mf *2nd time - Guitar solo*

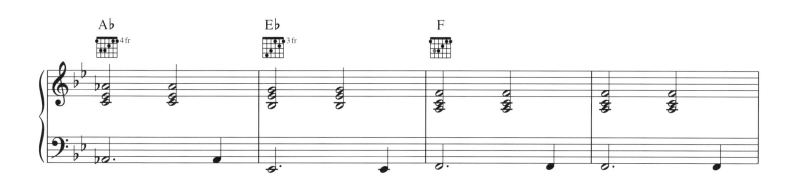

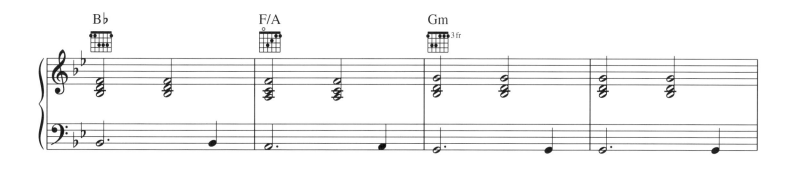

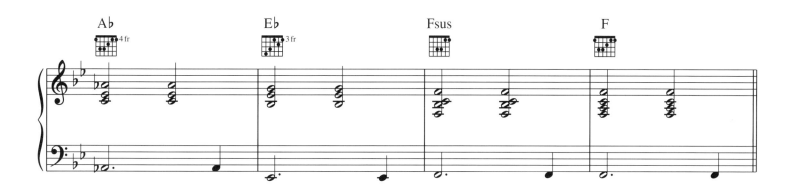

FLY LIKE AN EAGLE

Words and Music by
STEVE MILLER

GIMME SOME LOVIN'

Words and Music by STEVE WINWOOD,
MUFF WINWOOD and SPENCER DAVIS

HIGHER LOVE

Words and Music by WILL JENNINGS
and STEVE WINWOOD

I could light the night up with my
soul on fire. I could make the sun-shine from
pure de-sire. Let me feel that
love come o-ver me. Let me feel how

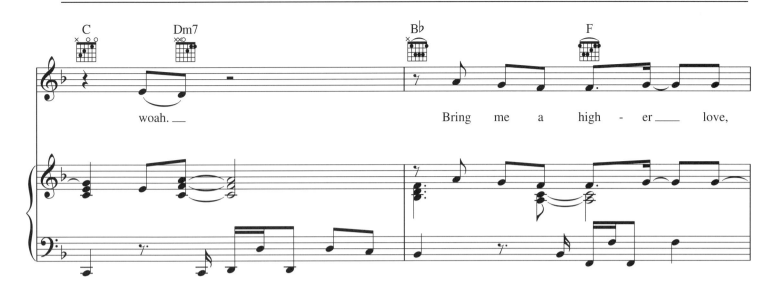

woah. ___ Bring me a high - er ___ love,

bring me a high - er ___ love. ___

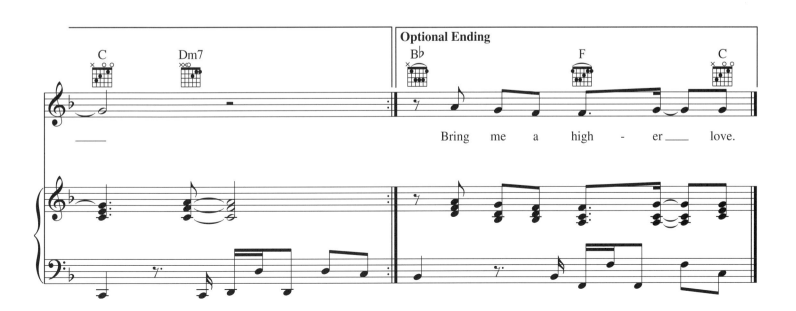

___ Bring me a high - er ___ love.

HOLD ON LOOSELY

Words and Music by DON BARNES,
JEFF CARLISI and JAMES MICHAEL PETERIK

HUSH

Words and Music by
JOE SOUTH

Driving Rock

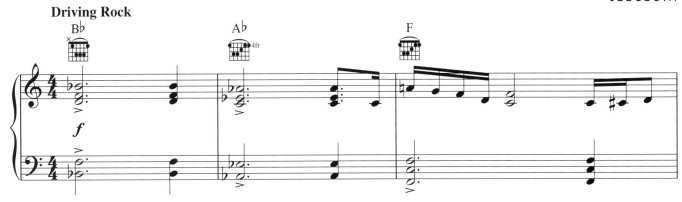

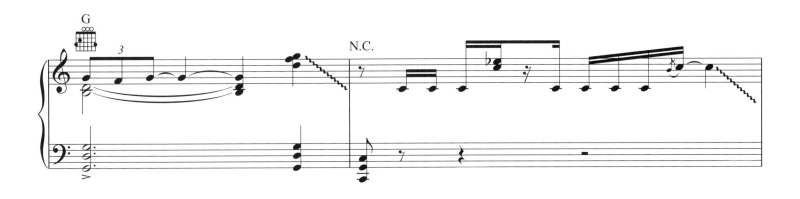

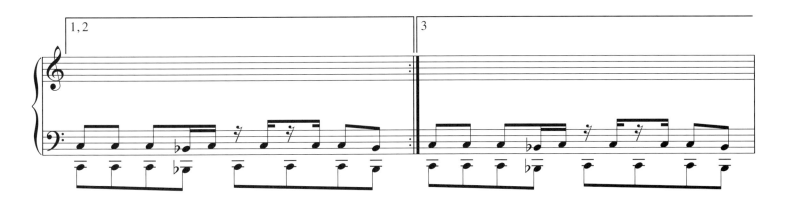

164

I DON'T WANT TO KNOW

Words and Music by
STEVIE NICKS

Moderately

I don't want to know the rea-sons why___ love keeps___ ___ right on___ walk-in' on down the line. I don't want to stand 'tween you and love. Hon-ey, I just___ want you to feel___ fine.___

I WANNA GO BACK

Words and Music by MONTY BYROM,
IRA WALKER and DANIEL CHAUNCEY

I
I re- call___ was list-'nin' to the ra- di- o.___
hang-in' out on Fri- day night.___

I LOVE ROCK 'N ROLL

Words and Music by ALAN MERRILL
and JAKE HOOKER

Lyrics:
I saw him danc - ing there ___ by the rec - ord ma -
smiled, so I got up ___ and asked ___ for his

I'D LOVE TO CHANGE THE WORLD

Words and Music by
ALVIN LEE

them and us, ___   stop the war. _

I'd

D.S. al Coda

CODA

rit.

I'M JUST A SINGER
(In a Rock and Roll Band)

Words and Music by
JOHN LODGE

With a driving rhythm

IN THE AIR TONIGHT

Words and Music by
PHIL COLLINS

LIGHTS

Words and Music by STEVE PERRY
and NEAL SCHON

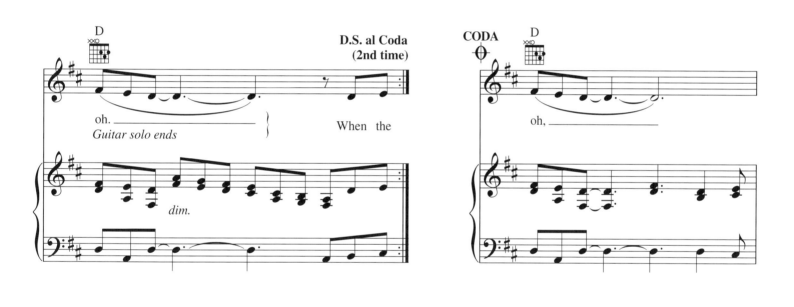

JUMP

Words and Music by DAVID LEE ROTH, EDWARD VAN HALEN,
ALEX VAN HALEN and MICHAEL ANTHONY

Jump!

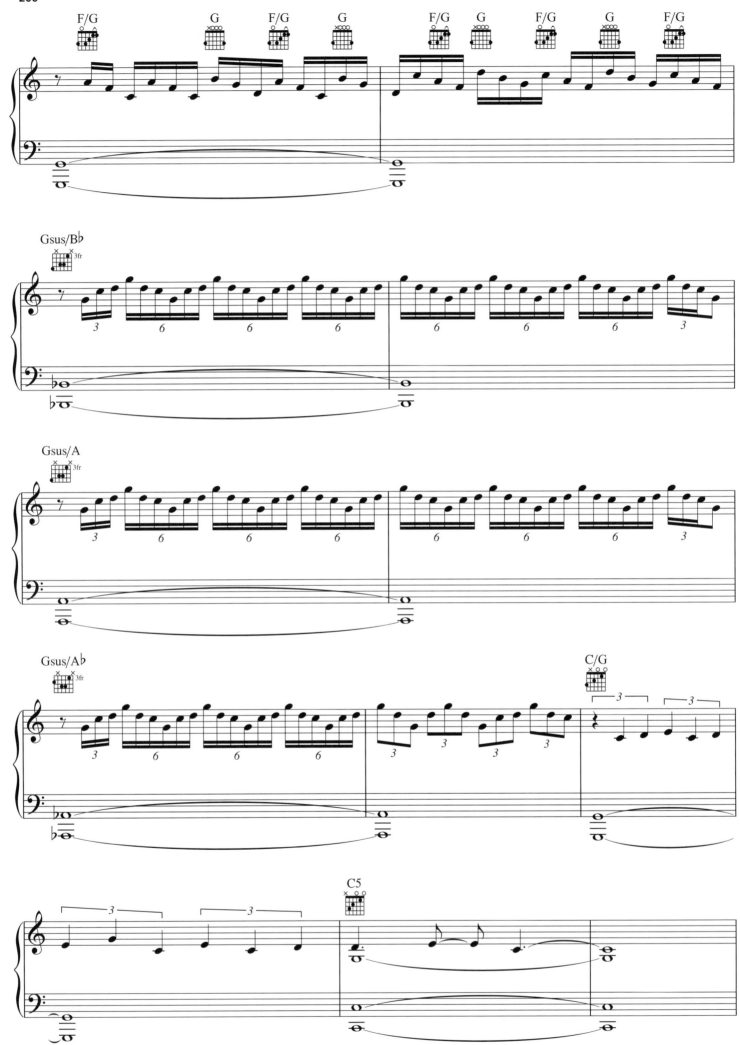

LA GRANGE

Words and Music by BILLY F GIBBONS,
DUSTY HILL and FRANK BEARD

LADY MADONNA

Words and Music by JOHN LENNON
and PAUL McCARTNEY

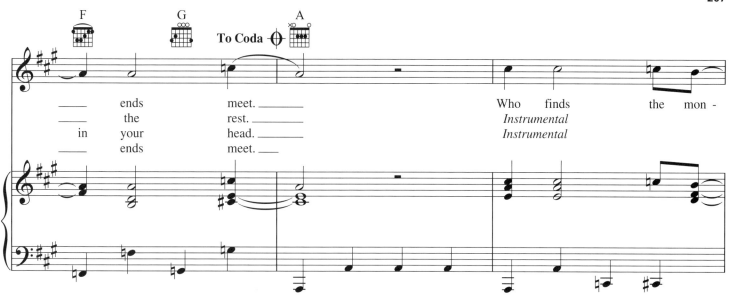

ends meet. _____
the rest. _____
in your head. _____
ends meet. _____

Who finds the mon-
Instrumental
Instrumental

-ey when you pay the rent? ___

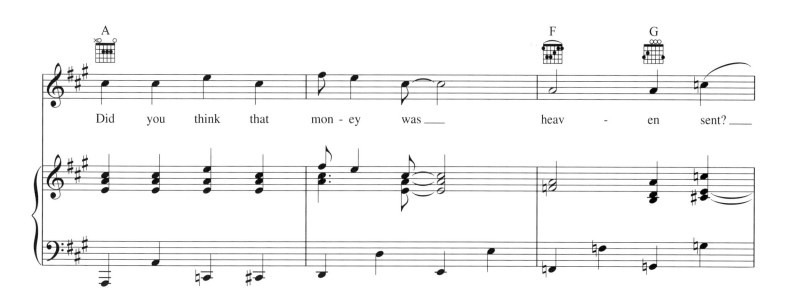

Did you think that mon-ey was ___ heav-en sent? ___

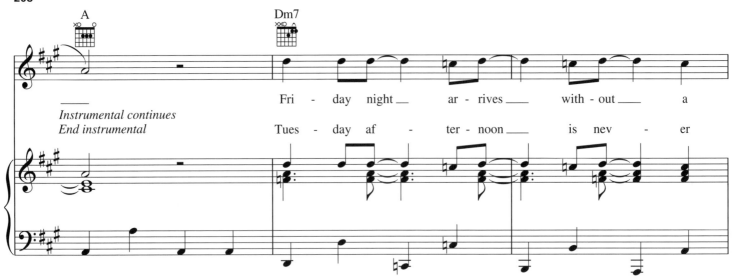

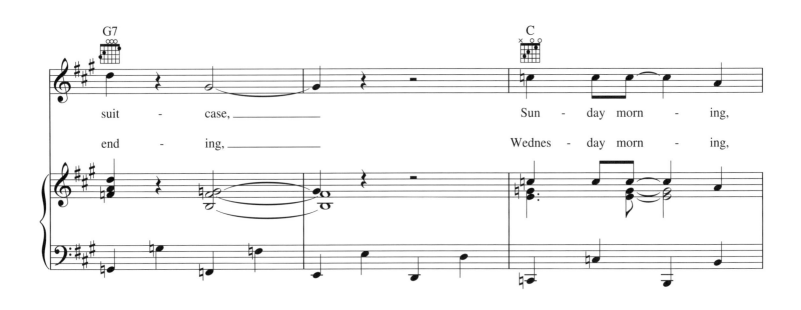

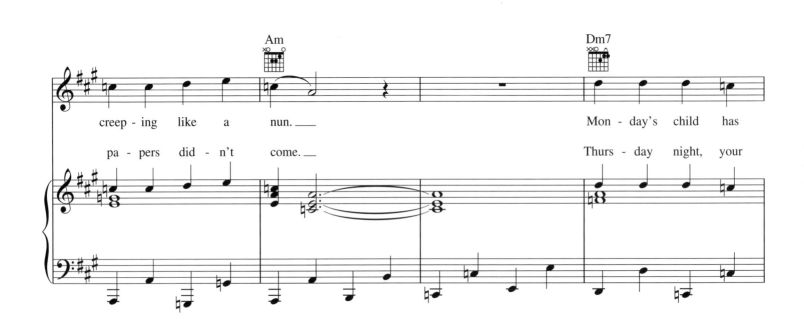

LAY DOWN SALLY

Words and Music by ERIC CLAPTON,
MARCY LEVY and GEORGE TERRY

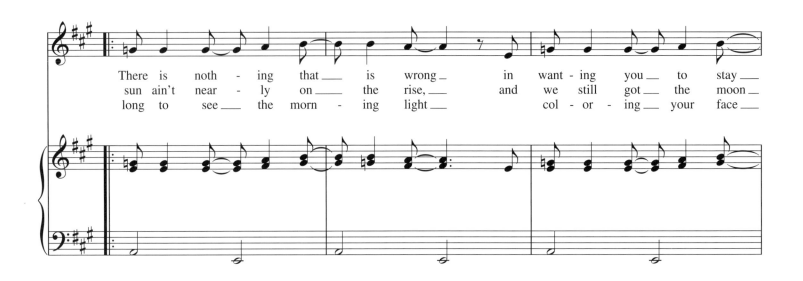

There is noth - ing that ___ is wrong ___ in want - ing you ___ to stay ___
sun ain't near - ly on ___ the rise, ___ and we still got ___ the moon ___
long to see ___ the morn - ing light ___ col - or - ing your face ___

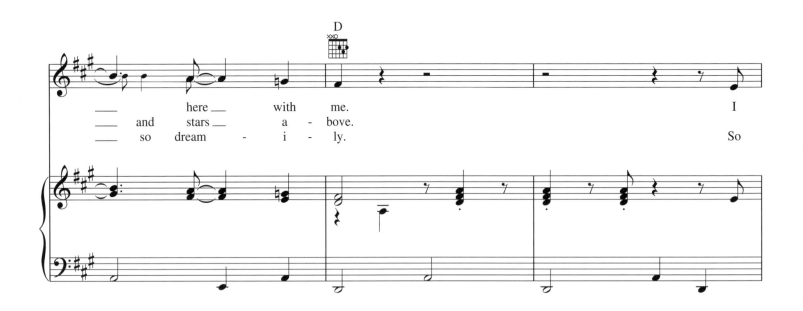

___ here ___ with me.   I
___ and stars ___ a - bove.   So
___ so dream - i - ly.

The talk to you. ___
I

D.S. al Coda

CODA

talk to you. ___

Repeat and Fade

LIVIN' ON A PRAYER

Words and Music by JON BON JOVI,
RICHIE SAMBORA and DESMOND CHILD

Moderate Rock

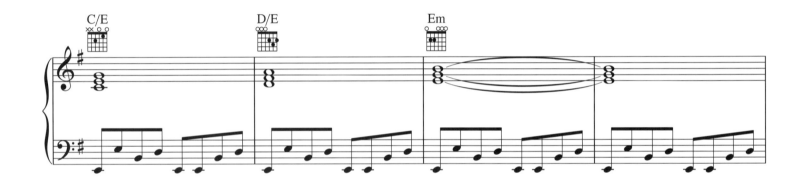

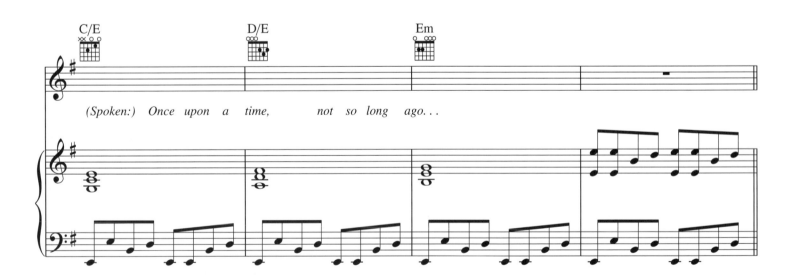

(Spoken:) Once upon a time, not so long ago...

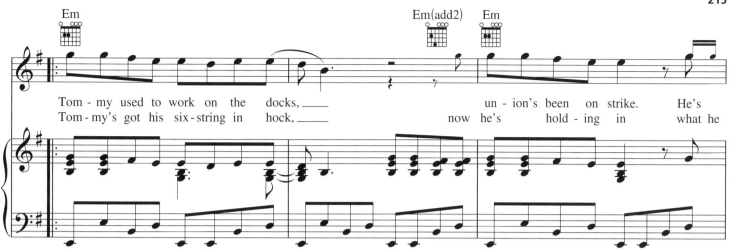

Tom - my used to work on the docks, _____ un - ion's been on strike. He's
Tom - my's got his six - string in hock, _____ now he's hold - ing in what he

down on his luck, it's tough, _____ so tough. _
used to make it talk. So tough, _____ it's tough. _

_____ Gi - na works the di - ner all day _____
_____ Gi - na dreams of run - ning a - way; _

THE LOGICAL SONG

Words and Music by RICK DAVIES
and ROGER HODGSON

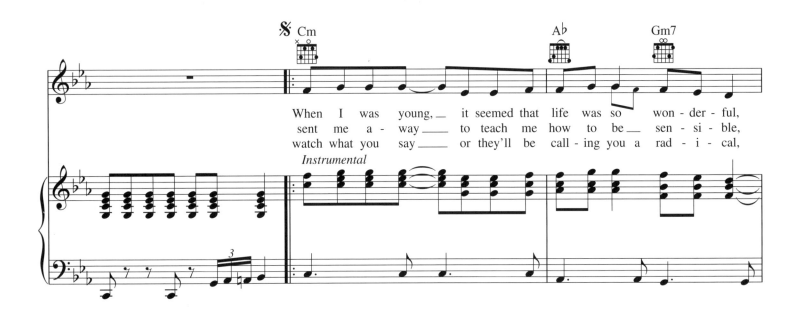

When I was young,__ it seemed that life was so won-der-ful,
sent me a-way__ to teach me how to be__ sen-si-ble,
watch what you say__ or they'll be call-ing you a rad-i-cal,

Instrumental

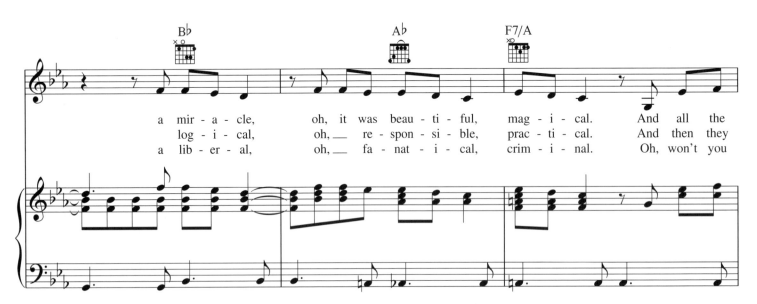

a mir-a-cle, oh, it was beau-ti-ful, mag-i-cal. And all the
log-i-cal, oh,__ re-spon-si-ble, prac-ti-cal. And then they
a lib-er-al, oh,__ fa-nat-i-cal, crim-i-nal. Oh, won't you

LONELY OL' NIGHT

Words and Music by
JOHN MELLENCAMP

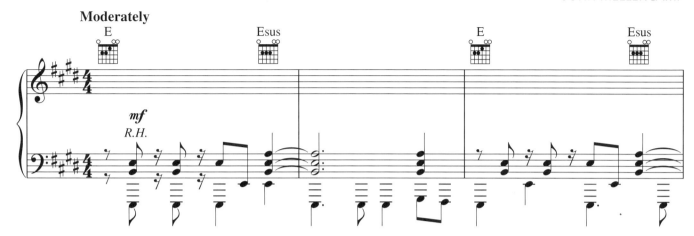

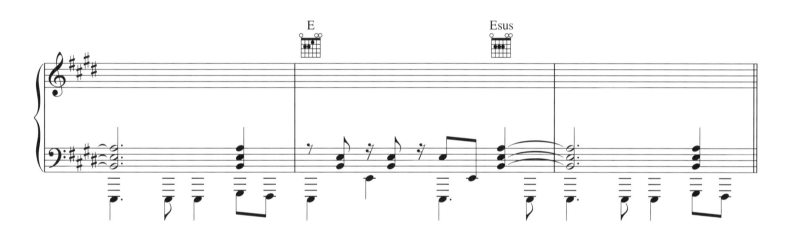

She calls me up and says, "Ba - by, it's a lone - ly ol' night." _____
Ra - di - o play - in' soft - ly some sing - er's sad, sad song. _____

I don't know, ___ I'm just so scared and lone-ly all at ___
He's sing-in' a-bout stand-in' in the shad-ows of love. _ I guess he feels _

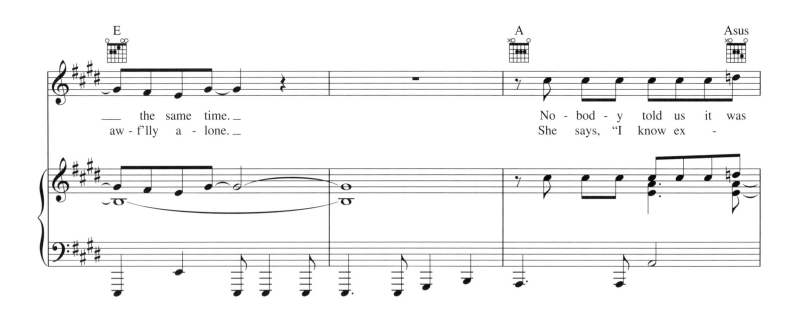

___ the same time. _ No - bod - y told us it was
aw - f'lly a - lone. _ She says, "I know ex -

gon - na work out ___ this way, _____ no no no no no. ___
act - ly what _ he means, _____ yeah yeah yeah yeah yeah." _

LOW RIDER

Words and Music by SYLVESTER ALLEN,
HAROLD R. BROWN, MORRIS DICKERSON, JERRY GOLDSTEIN,
LEROY JORDAN, LEE OSKAR, CHARLES W. MILLER and HOWARD SCOTT

To Coda

1. 2.

Low rid - er drives a lit-tle slow - er, The
Low rid - er knows ev 'ry street, yeah!

3.

low rid - er is a re-al go - er.
low rid - er is the one to meet, yeah! Low rid -

232

NOTHING'S GONNA STOP US NOW

Words and Music by DIANE WARREN
and ALBERT HAMMOND

MAGGIE MAY

Words and Music by ROD STEWART
and MARTIN QUITTENTON

Additional Lyrics

2. You lured me away from home, just to save you from being alone.
   You stole my soul, that's a pain I can do without.
   All I needed was a friend to lend a guiding hand.
   But you turned into a lover, and, Mother, what a lover! You wore me out.
   All you did was wreck my bed and in the morning kick me in the head.
   Oh, Maggie, I couldn't have tried any more.

3. You lured me away from home 'cause you didn't want to be alone.
   You stole my heart, I couldn't leave you if I tried.
    I suppose I could collect my books and get back to school,
   Or steal my Daddy's cue and make a living out of playing pool,
   Or find myself a rock and roll band that needs a helpin' hand.
   Oh, Maggie, I wish I'd never seen your face. *(To Coda)*

MIDNIGHT RIDER

Words and Music by GREGG ALLMAN
and ROBERT KIM PAYNE

Moderate Southern Rock

Guitar solo

Solo ends

MONDAY, MONDAY

Words and Music by
JOHN PHILLIPS

Moderately

1,3. Mon - day, Mon - day, so good to me
2. Mon - day, Mon - day, Can't trust that day

Mon - day morn - in', it was all I hoped it would be.
Mon - day, Mon - day, some - times it just turns out that way.

Oh, Mon - day morn - in', Mon - day morn - in' could-n't guar - an - tee
Oh, Mon - day morn - in', you give me no warn - in' of what was to be

MY SWEET LORD

Words and Music by
GEORGE HARRISON

ONCE BITTEN TWICE SHY

Moderate Rock Beat

Words and Music by
IAN HUNTER

Well the times are get-tin' hard for you __ lit-tle girl. I'm a
mid-dle of the night on the o-pen road. __ The
wom-an you're a mess, gon-na die in your sleep. There's

Instrumental

OWNER OF A LONELY HEART

Words and Music by TREVOR HORN,
JON ANDERSON, TREVOR RABIN and CHRIS SQUIRE

PINBALL WIZARD

Words and Music by
PETE TOWNSHEND

REELING IN THE YEARS

Words and Music by WALTER BECKER
and DONALD FAGEN

RENEGADE

Words and Music by
TOMMY SHAW

Moderately
N.C.

Oh _ mam-ma I'm in fear for my life from the long _ arm _ of the law. _
Law - man has put an end to my run-ning and I'm so far _ from my home. _

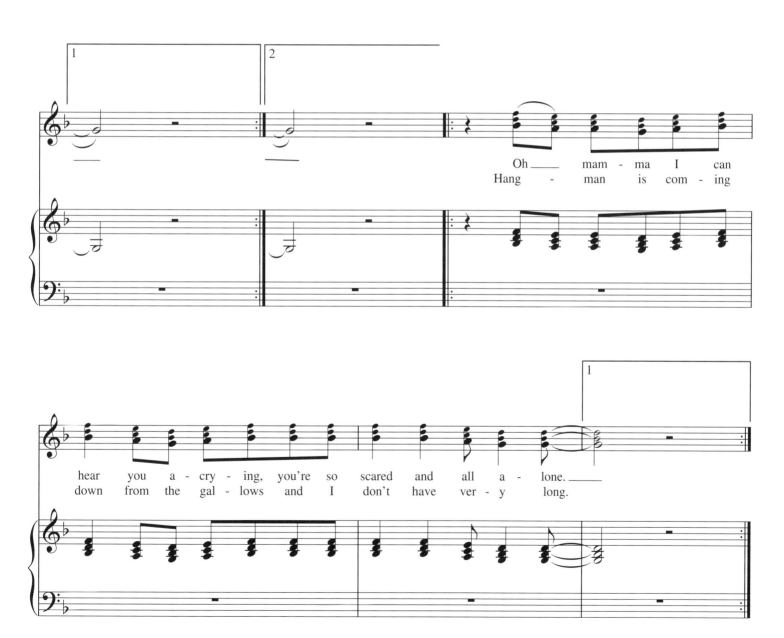

Oh _ mam-ma I can
Hang - man is com - ing

hear you a-cry - ing, you're so scared and all a - lone. _
down from the gal - lows and I don't have ver-y long.

To Coda

Oh mam-ma I've been years on the lam___ and had a
high price on my head. _____ Law-man said get him
dead or a-live,___ now it's for sure he'll see me___ dead. ___
Dear mam-ma I can hear you a-cry-ing,___ you're so___

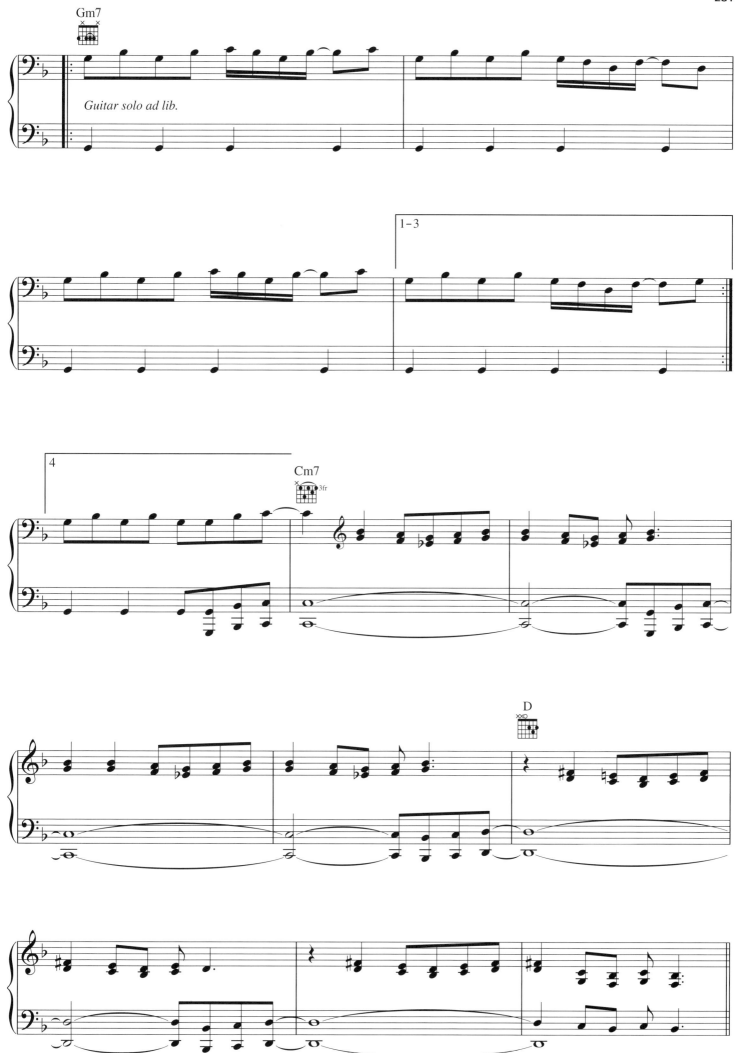

ROCK AND ROLL HOOCHIE KOO

Words and Music by
RICK DERRINGER

could-n't stop mov-ing when it first took hold. _____
qui-tos start-ed buzz-ing 'bout this time of year. _____
hope you all know what I'm talk-in' a-bout. _____

It was a warm spring night at the old town hall.
I'm go-ing out back, said she'll meet me there.
The way they wig-gle that thing real-ly knocks me out.

There was a band called "The Jok-ers," they were
We were roll-ing in the grass that grows be-
Get-tin' high all the time, hope you

ROCK THE CASBAH

Words and Music by JOE STRUMMER,
MICK JONES and TOPPER HEADON

(She's)
SOME KIND OF WONDERFUL

Words and Music by
JOHN ELLISON

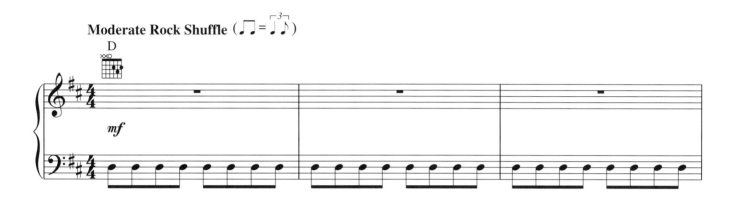

I don't need _____ a whole lot's of mon - ey. I don't need _____
_____ her in my arms _____ you know she

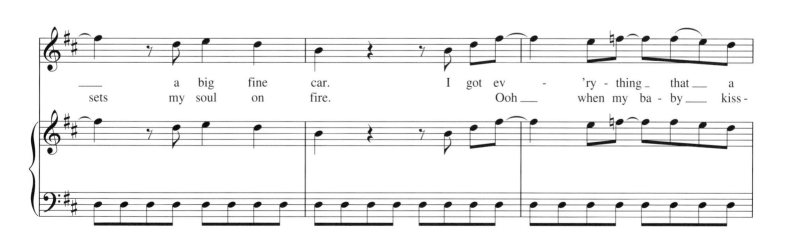

_____ a big fine car. I got ev - 'ry - thing _____ that _____ a
sets my soul on fire. Ooh _____ when my ba - by _____ kiss-

man could want. I got more ____ than I could ask ____
es me ____ my heart be - comes filled with ____ de -

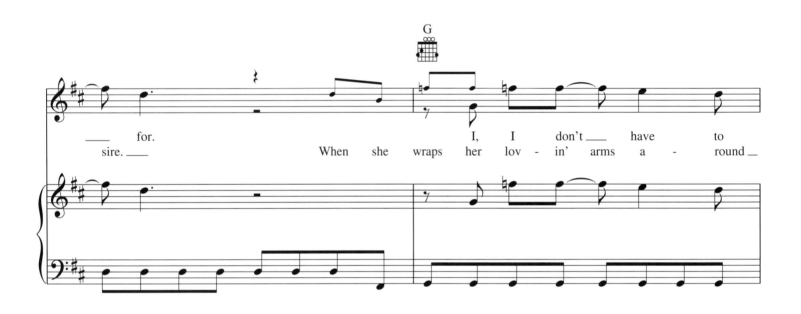

G

____ for.
sire. ____ When she wraps her lov - in' arms a - round ____

I, I don't ____ have to

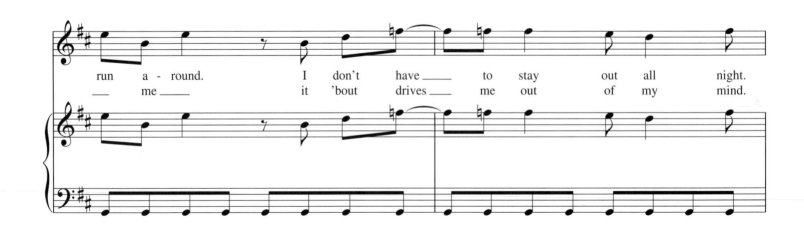

run a - round. I don't have ____ to stay out all night.
____ me ____ it 'bout drives ____ me out of my mind.

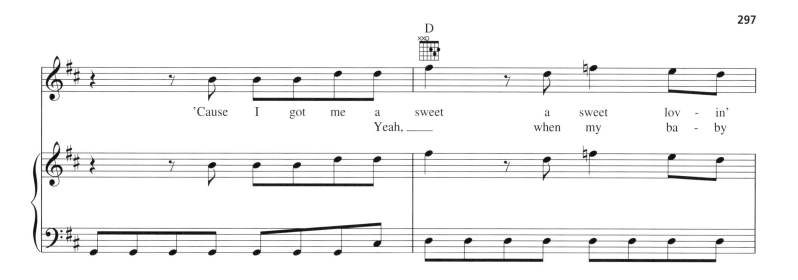

'Cause I got me a sweet _____ a sweet lov - in'
Yeah, _____ when my ba - by

wom - an _____ and she knows _____ just how to treat me right. _____
kiss - es me, _____ chills _____ run up and down my spine. _____

Well, my ba - by, she's al - right.

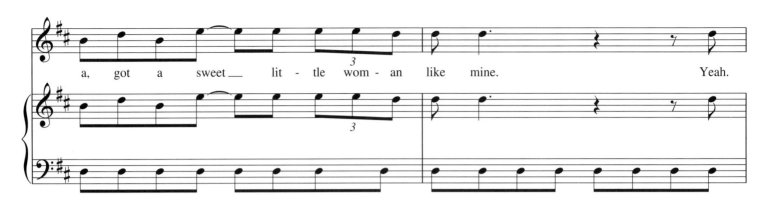

a, got a sweet __ lit - tle wom - an like mine. Yeah.

Now can I get a wit - ness? Can I get a

Bm

wit - ness? Well, can I get a

D   Bm

wit - ness?   Can I get a wit - ness?

ROCKY MOUNTAIN WAY

Words and Music by JOE WALSH, JOE VITALE,
KEN PASSARELLI and ROCKE GRACE

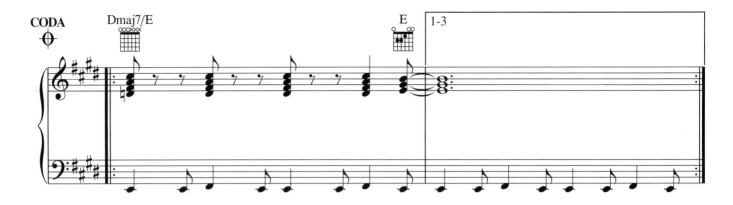

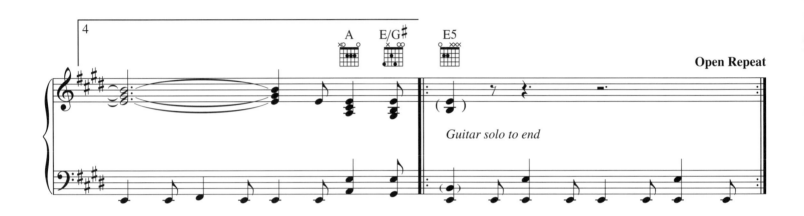

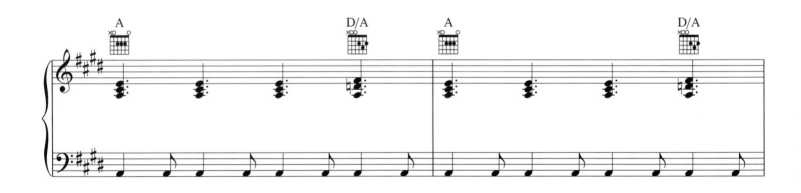

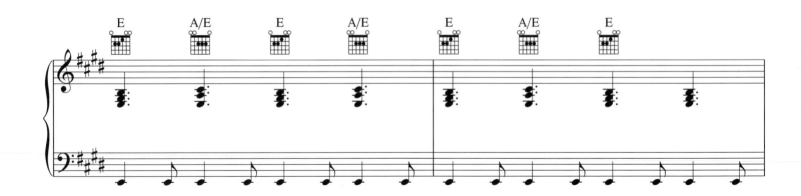

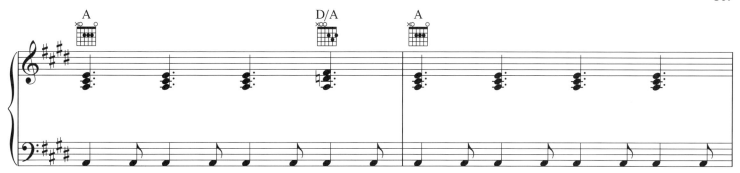

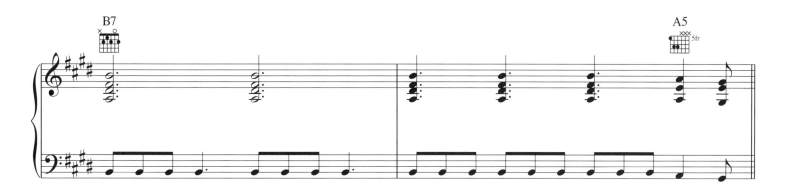

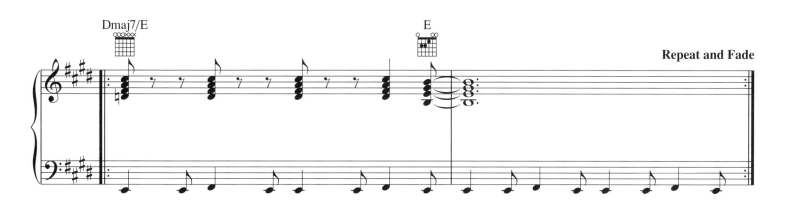

Repeat and Fade

Optional Ending

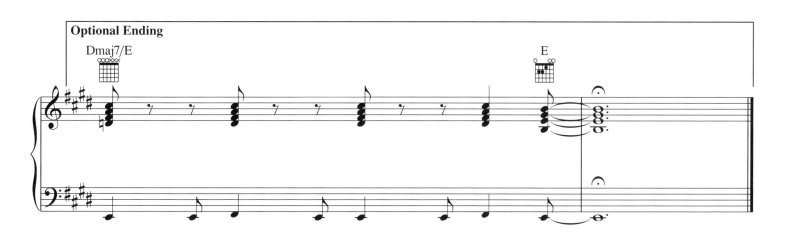

SPINNING WHEEL

Words and Music by
DAVID CLAYTON THOMAS

STAYIN' ALIVE

from the Motion Picture SATURDAY NIGHT FEVER

Words and Music by ROBIN GIBB,
MAURICE GIBB and BARRY GIBB

WALK THIS WAY

Words and Music by STEVEN TYLER
and JOE PERRY

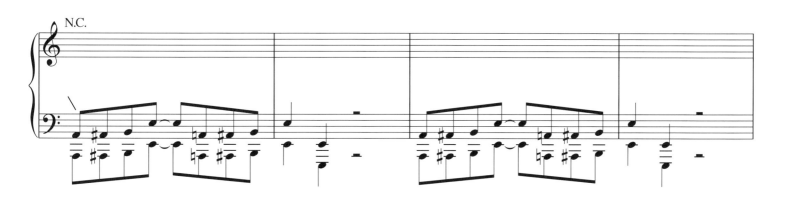

STEPPIN' OUT

Words and Music by
JOE JACKSON

*Recorded a half step higher.

THE STROKE

Words and Music by
BILLY SQUIER

TEMPTED

Words and Music by CHRISTOPHER DIFFORD
and GLENN TILBROOK

*Recorded a half step lower.

TURN THE PAGE

Words and Music by
BOB SEGER

Moderately

1. On a long and lone-some high-way __ east of O - ma-ha __ you can
2., 3. (*See additional lyrics*)

lis - ten to the en - gine moan-in' out its one __ note song, you can

think a - bout __ the wom - an __ or the girl you knew __ the night __ be -

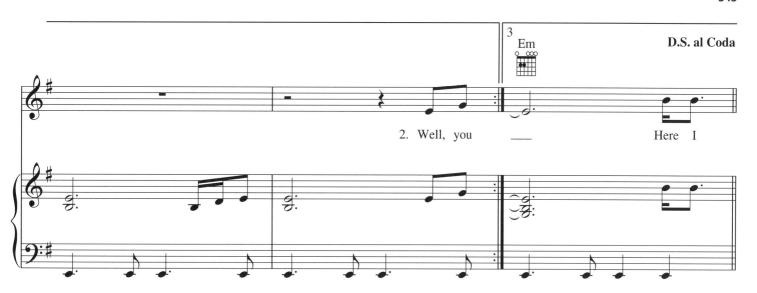

2. Well, you ___ Here I

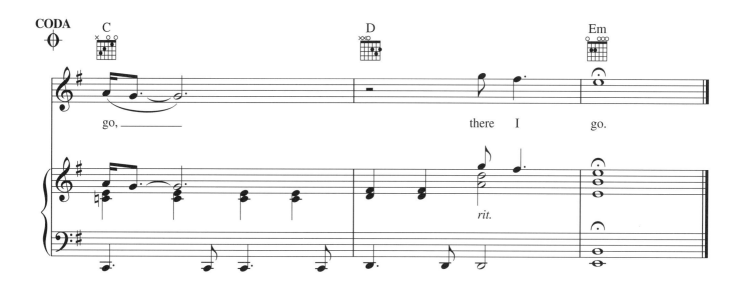

CODA

go, ___ there I go.

rit.

Additional Lyrics

2. Well, you walk into a restaurant strung out from the road
   And you feel the eyes upon you as you're shakin' off the cold;
   You pretend it doesn't bother you but you just want to explode.
   Most times you can't hear 'em talk, other times you can,
   All the same old cliches, "Is that a woman or a man?"
   And you always seem out numbered, you don't dare make a stand.
   Chorus

3. Out there in the spotlight you're a million miles away.
   Every ounce of energy you try to give away
   As the sweat pours out your body like the music that you play.
   Later in the evening as you lie awake in bed
   With the echoes from the amplifiers ringing in your head,
   You smoke the day's last cigarette remembering what she said.
   Chorus

WALKING IN MEMPHIS

Words and Music by
MARC COHN

WE DIDN'T START THE FIRE

Words and Music by
BILLY JOEL

Har-ry Tru-man, Dor-is Day, Red Chi - na, John-nie Ray,

South Pac- if - ic, Wal - ter Win-chell, Joe Di - Mag - gi - o. Joe Mc-Car - thy, Rich-ard Nix-on,

Stu - de- bak - er, Tel - e - vi - sion, North Ko - re - a, South Ko - re - a, Mar - i - lyn Mon - roe.

WEREWOLVES OF LONDON

Words and Music by WARREN ZEVON,
ROBERT WACHTEL and LeROY MARINEL

WHAT'S LOVE GOT TO DO WITH IT

Words and Music by TERRY BRITTE
and GRAHAM LYLE

Slow Rock

You must un-der-stand,___ though the touch of__ your hand__ Makes my
may seem__ to you___ that I'm act-ing__ con-fused___ When you're

pulse re-act___
close to me___

That it's on-ly___ the thrill___ of
If I tend to__ look dazed___ I

boy meet-ing girl___ op-po-sites at-tract___ it's
read it__ some-place___ I got cause to__ be___ there's a

WHITE WEDDING

Words and Music by
BILLY IDOL

Fast Rock

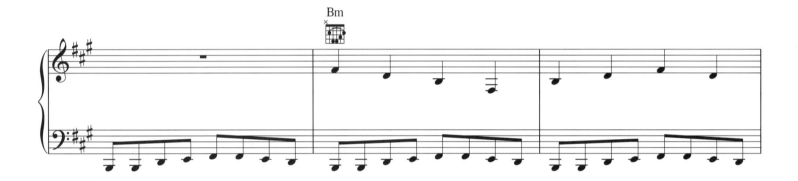

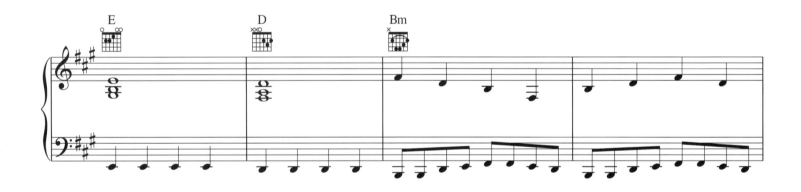

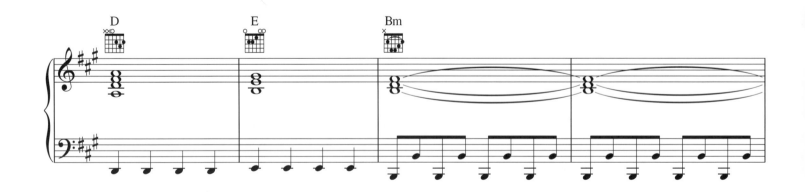

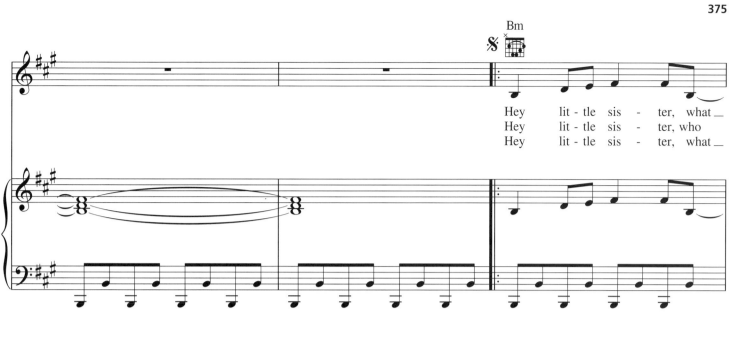

Hey lit - tle sis - ter, what __
Hey lit - tle sis - ter, who
Hey lit - tle sis - ter, what __

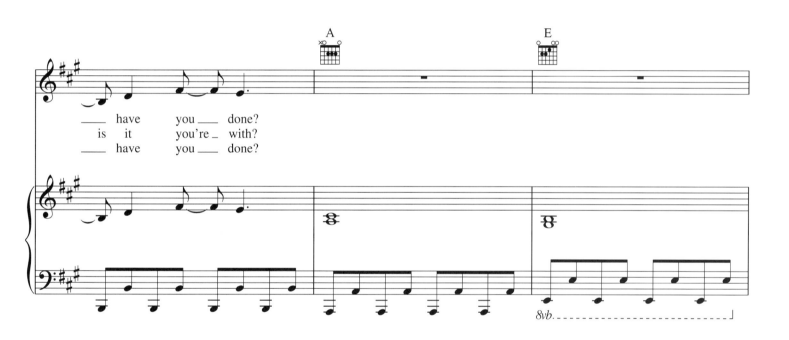

__ have you __ done?
is it you're __ with?
__ have you __ done?

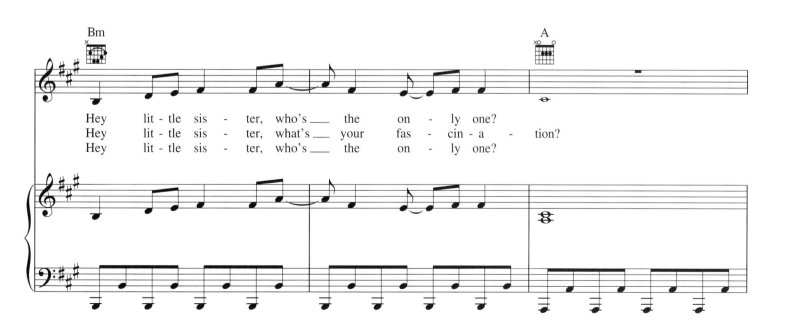

Hey lit - tle sis - ter, who's __ the on - ly one?
Hey lit - tle sis - ter, what's __ your fas - cin - a - tion?
Hey lit - tle sis - ter, who's __ the on - ly one?

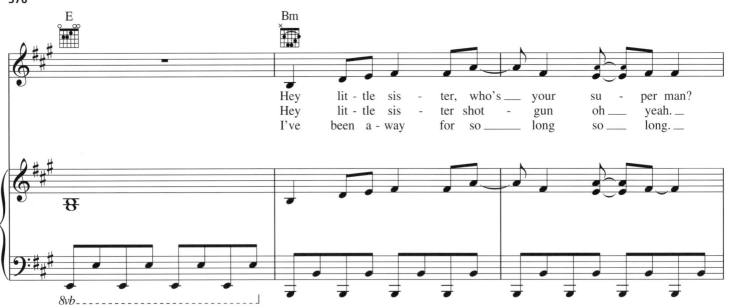

Hey lit - tle sis - ter, who's __ your su - per man?
Hey lit - tle sis - ter shot - gun oh yeah. __
I've been a - way for so __ long so __ long. __

Hey lit - tle sis - ter, who's __ the one __ you want? Hey lit - tle sis - ter, shot-
Hey lit - tle sis - ter who's __ your su - per man? Hey lit - tle sis - ter shot-
I've been a - way for so __ long so __ long. __ I let you go for so __

- gun! }
- gun! } It's a nice day to start __ a - gain.
__ long. }

A WHITER SHADE OF PALE

Words and Music by KEITH REID
and GARY BROOKER

We skipped the light ____ fan - dan - go,
She said, "I'm home ____ on shore leave,"
She said, "There is ____ no rea - son, ____

WORKING FOR THE WEEKEND

Words and Music by PAUL DEAN,
MATTHEW FRENETTE and MICHAEL RENO

WRAPPED AROUND YOUR FINGER

Music and Lyrics by
STING

YOU REALLY GOT ME

Words and Music by
RAY DAVIES

YOUNG AMERICANS

Words and Music by
DAVID BOWIE

Big Books of Music

Our "Big Books" feature big selections of popular titles under one cover, perfect for performing musicians, music aficionados or the serious hobbyist. All books are arranged for piano, voice, and guitar, and feature stay-open binding, so the books lie flat without breaking the spine.

BIG BOOK OF BALLADS
63 songs.
00310485 ....$19.95

BIG BOOK OF BIG BAND HITS
84 songs.
00310701 ....$19.95

BIG BOOK OF BROADWAY
70 songs.
00311658 ....$19.95

BIG BOOK OF CHILDREN'S SONGS
55 songs.
00359261 ....$14.95

GREAT BIG BOOK OF CHILDREN'S SONGS
74 songs.
00310002 ....$14.95

FANTASTIC BIG BOOK OF CHILDREN'S SONGS
67 songs.
00311062 ....$16.95

MIGHTY BIG BOOK OF CHILDREN'S SONGS
65 songs.
00310467 ....$14.95

REALLY BIG BOOK OF CHILDREN'S SONGS
63 songs.
00310372 ....$15.95

BIG BOOK OF CHILDREN'S MOVIE SONGS
66 songs.
00310731 ....$17.95

BIG BOOK OF CHRISTMAS SONGS
126 songs.
00311520 ....$19.95

BIG BOOK OF CLASSIC ROCK
77 songs.
00310801 ....$19.95

BIG BOOK OF CLASSICAL MUSIC
100 songs.
00310508 ....$19.95

BIG BOOK OF CONTEMPORARY CHRISTIAN FAVORITES
50 songs.
00310021 ....$19.95

BIG BOOK OF COUNTRY MUSIC
63 songs.
00310188 ....$19.95

BIG BOOK OF DISCO & FUNK
70 songs.
00310878 ....$19.95

BIG BOOK OF EARLY ROCK N' ROLL
99 songs.
00310398 ....$19.95

BIG BOOK OF FOLK POP ROCK
80 songs.
00311125 ....$19.95

BIG BOOK OF GOSPEL SONGS
100 songs.
00310604 ....$19.95

BIG BOOK OF HYMNS
125 hymns.
00310510 ....$17.95

BIG BOOK OF IRISH SONGS
76 songs.
00310981 ....$16.95

BIG BOOK OF JAZZ
75 songs.
00311557 ....$19.95

BIG BOOK OF LATIN AMERICAN SONGS
89 songs.
00311562 ....$19.95

BIG BOOK OF LOVE SONGS
80 songs.
00310784 ....$19.95

BIG BOOK OF MOTOWN
84 songs.
00311061 ....$19.95

BIG BOOK OF MOVIE MUSIC
72 songs.
00311582 ....$19.95

BIG BOOK OF NOSTALGIA
160 songs.
00310004 ....$19.95

BIG BOOK OF OLDIES
73 songs.
00310756 ....$19.95

BIG BOOK OF RHYTHM & BLUES
67 songs.
00310169 ....$19.95

BIG BOOK OF ROCK
78 songs.
00311566 ....$19.95

BIG BOOK OF SOUL
71 songs.
00310771 ....$19.95

BIG BOOK OF STANDARDS
86 songs.
00311667 ....$19.95

BIG BOOK OF SWING
84 songs.
00310359 ....$19.95

BIG BOOK OF TORCH SONGS
75 songs.
00310561 ....$19.95

BIG BOOK OF TV THEME SONGS
78 songs.
00310504 ....$19.95

BIG BOOK OF WEDDING MUSIC
77 songs.
00311567 ....$19.95

0105

THE POP/ROCK ERA

Hal Leonard is proud to present these fantastic folios that gather the best popular songs from the '50s to today! All books arranged for piano, voice, and guitar.

THE POP/ROCK ERA: THE '50s

54 highlights from the first official decade of the pop/rock revolution, including: All Shook Up • At the Hop • Don't Be Cruel (To a Heart That's True) • Donna • Get a Job • Great Balls of Fire • Hound Dog • It's So Easy • Kansas City • (You've Got) Personality • That'll Be the Day • Why Do Fools Fall in Love • and more.
00310788..$14.95

THE POP/ROCK ERA: THE '60s

52 songs that helped shape the pop/rock era, including: Baby Love • Can't Take My Eyes off of You • Crying • Fun, Fun, Fun • Hey Jude • I Heard It Through the Grapevine • I Think We're Alone Now • Louie, Louie • Mony, Mony • Respect • Stand by Me • Stop! In the Name of Love • Wooly Bully • and more.
00310789..$14.95

THE POP/ROCK ERA: THE '70s

44 of the top songs from the '70s, including: ABC • Baby, I Love Your Way • Bohemian Rhapsody • Don't Cry Out Loud • Fire and Rain • I Love the Night Life • Imagine • Joy to the World • Just My Imagination (Running Away with Me) • The Logical Song • Oye Como Va • Piano Man • Three Times a Lady • We've Only Just Begun • You Are So Beautiful • and more.
00310790..$14.95

THE POP/ROCK ERA: THE '80s

38 top pop hits from the '80s, including: Back in the High Life Again • Centerfold • Every Breath You Take • Eye in the Sky • Higher Love •Summer of '69 • Sweet Dreams (Are Made of This) • Thriller • Time After Time • and more.
0031079..$14.95

THE POP/ROCK ERA: THE '90s

35 hits that shaped pop music in the 1990s, including: All I Wanna Do • Angel • Come to My Window • (Everything I Do) I Do It for You • Fields of Gold • From a Distance • Hard to Handle • Hero • I Will Remember You • Mambo No. 5 (A Little Bit Of...) • My Heart Will Go On (Love Theme from 'Titanic') • Ray of Light • Tears in Heaven • When She Cries • and more.
00310792..$14.95

Prices, contents and availability subject to change without notice.